Chameleons

Victoria Blakemore

vblakemore.author@gmail.com

Copyright info/picture credits

Cover, Anneke/AdobeStock; Page 3, Silvo/Pixabay; Page 5, mailgifson/AdobeStock; Page 7, Arcaion/Pixabay; Page 9, cyberangel70/Pixabay; Page 11, Fix-Foxi/Pixabay; Pages 12-13, skeeze/Pixabay; Page 15, Cathy Keifer/AdobeStock; Page 17, Gellinger/Pixabay; Page 19, onkelramirez1/Pixabay; Page 21, nandhukumar/Pixabay; Page 23; Free-Photos/Pixabay; Page 25, Rodrigo_Souza/Pixabay; Page 27, Jan/AdobeStock; Page 29, Arcaion/Pixabay; Page 31, jmby/Pixabay; Page 33, Anneke/AdobeStock

Table of Contents

What Are Chameleons?

Chameleons are reptiles.

They are cold-blooded

vertebrates.

There are over 160 different

kinds of chameleons. They

differ in their coloring, size,

and where they live.

Chameleons are known for their **ability** to change colors.

Size

There are many kinds of chameleons. Different kinds of chameleons can be different sizes.

Smaller chameleons are only a few inches long. Other kinds can grow to be up to three feet in length.

The Brookesia-micra is the world's smallest chameleon. It is less than an inch long. It is only found on the island of Madagascar.

Physical Characteristics

Chameleons have a special **prehensile** tail. They can use it to grip branches. This lets them be very good climbers.

As chameleons grow, they need to shed their skin. They shed it in small pieces. They do not shed it all at once like snakes.

Chameleons are able to see all the way around their body. They can see in two different directions at the same time.

Changing Colors

Chameleons have special crystal-like pieces in their scales. This lets them change colors.

They change color due to temperature, mood, and their surroundings. Their color changes help them to communicate and to stay safe from predators.

Chameleon scales are different colors. They can change colors, but not patterns.

Habitat

Chameleons can live in several different habitats. They can be found in rainforests, savannas, and in deserts.

Most kinds of chameleons live in trees or bushes. There are some that live on the ground, especially in the desert.

Range

Chameleons are found in parts of Asia, Europe, North America, and Africa.

Most chameleons are found in
Madagascar, an island off the
coast of Africa.

Diet

Chameleons are **omnivores**.
They eat both meat and
plants.

Their diet is made up of
insects, lizards, small birds,
fruit, and leaves.

They have a very long, sticky
tongue that they use to catch
prey. Their tongue can be
longer than their body. 15

Communication

The main way that chameleons communicate with each other is through the color of their skin.

They can change their skin color to show their mood. This lets other chameleons know if they should stay away.

Like some other reptiles,

chameleons cannot make

sounds to communicate.

Movement

Chameleons move in an odd way. Their movements are very **jerky**.

Researchers believe that chameleons do this as a form of **camouflage**. They **mimic** the movements of leaves.

Chameleons move very slowly when they are hunting. They like to sneak up on their prey.

19

Chameleon Life

Chameleons are **solitary** animals. They spend most of their time alone.

They are **diurnal** animals. This means that they are most active during the day. This is the case for many cold-blooded animals.

While chameleons are usually active during the day, some may also be active at night.

Young Chameleons

Chameleons lay a **clutch** of about 20 eggs. Some can lay up to 100 eggs.

Mothers lay their eggs in a hole in the soil. Once the eggs hatch a few months later, the young chameleons are on their own to find food, shelter, and to avoid predators.

Young chameleons have many predators. Many do not survive the first few months.

Staying Warm

Like other reptiles, chameleons are **cold-blooded**. Their body does not create its own heat.

They have to warm themselves in the sun each day. If the temperature gets too low, they may change to a darker color. This is because darker colors **absorb** more heat.

Chameleons that are kept as pets need a special lamp to stay warm. It creates heat like the sun does.

Chameleons as Pets

Chameleons are often kept as pets. However, they can be hard to care for.

Chameleons can become stressed easily. They also need a lot of special care to keep them healthy.

Chameleons don't usually like to be picked up. They are not the right pets for people who want to hold their animals. **27**

Population

Chameleon populations have been **declining** in many parts of the world. There are some kinds of chameleons that are already **endangered**.

If populations keep declining, many more chameleons will soon be endangered.

In the wild, chameleons can live for several years. There are some kinds that only live a few months.

Helping Chameleons

The Chameleon Specialist Group is a group of experts from all over the world. They are working to find ways to help wild chameleons.

They study chameleons in the wild to learn about them. They want to learn about chameleons so they can help them.

Another way they are trying to help is habitat **conservation**. Many habitats are being destroyed. If chameleon habitats are protected, they will have a safe place to live.

The Chameleon Specialist Group wants to save chameleons. They don't want them to become **extinct**.

Glossary

Ability: being able to do something

Absorb: to take in, soak up

Camouflage: when an animal blends in with their surroundings

Clutch: a group of eggs

Cold-blooded: an animal whose temperature changes with the air temperature

Conservation: protecting from loss or destruction

Declining: getting smaller

Diurnal: active during the day

Endangered: at risk of becoming extinct

Extinct: when there are no more of an animal left

Jerky: having sudden starts and stops

Mimic: to copy

Omnivore: an animal that eats meat and plants

Prehensile: able to grasp

Solitary: living alone

Vertebrate: an animal that has a backbone

About the Author

Victoria Blakemore is a first grade

teacher in Southwest Florida with a

passion for reading.

You can visit her at

www.elementaryexplorers.com

Also in This Series

Gray Wolves	Sloths	Flamingos	Camels	Koalas	Honey Bees	Pandas
Pangolins	White-Tailed Deer	Orcas	Giraffes	Corn	Meerkats	Echidnas
Walruses	Raccoons	Bald Eagles	Apples	Arctic Foxes	Red Pandas	Cassowaries
Tigers	Ladybugs	Moose	Beluga Whales	Leopards	Elephants	Jellyfish
Binturongs	Lions	Dolphins	Reindeer	Hammerhead Sharks	Hippos	Pumpkins
Peafowl	Chameleons	Florida Panthers	Aye-Ayes	Black Bears	Cheetahs	Manatees
Gingerbread	Polar Bears	Hot Chocolate	Orangutans	Coyotes	Marshmallows	Strawberries

Victoria Blakemore

Also in This Series

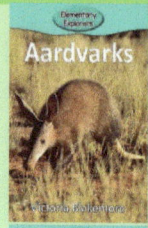

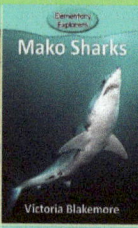

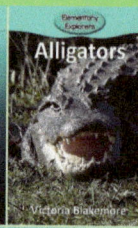

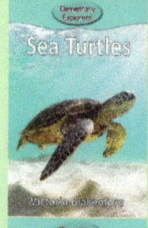

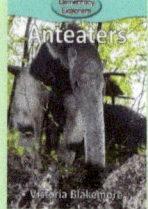

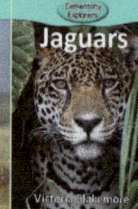

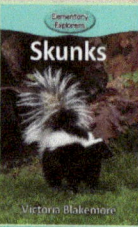

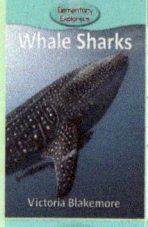

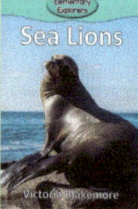

Aardvarks — Victoria Blakemore
Mako Sharks — Victoria Blakemore
Alligators — Victoria Blakemore
Frogs — Victoria Blakemore
Hedgehogs — Victoria Blakemore
Brown Bears — Victoria Blakemore
Bongos — Victoria Blakemore

Sea Turtles — Victoria Blakemore
Quokkas — Victoria Blakemore
Muskrats — Victoria Blakemore
Zebras — Victoria Blakemore
Red Foxes — Victoria Blakemore
Ring-Tailed Lemurs — Victoria Blakemore
Platypuses — Victoria Blakemore

Anteaters — Victoria Blakemore
Kangaroos — Victoria Blakemore
Rhinos — Victoria Blakemore
Jaguars — Victoria Blakemore
Wombats — Victoria Blakemore
Capybaras — Victoria Blakemore
Gorillas — Victoria Blakemore

Cats — Victoria Blakemore
Skunks — Victoria Blakemore
Butterflies — Victoria Blakemore
Dingoes — Victoria Blakemore
Snow Leopards — Victoria Blakemore
African Wild Dogs — Victoria Blakemore
Penguins — Victoria Blakemore

Whale Sharks — Victoria Blakemore
Wolverines — Victoria Blakemore
Warthogs — Victoria Blakemore
Caracals — Victoria Blakemore
Badgers — Victoria Blakemore
Seals — Victoria Blakemore
Hummingbirds — Victoria Blakemore

Pikas — Victoria Blakemore
Humpback Whales — Victoria Blakemore
Pumas — Victoria Blakemore
Lemonade — Victoria Blakemore
Llamas — Victoria Blakemore
Tulips — Victoria Blakemore
Ostriches — Victoria Blakemore

Sunflowers — Victoria Blakemore
Fennec Foxes — Victoria Blakemore
Sea Lions — Victoria Blakemore
Squirrels — Victoria Blakemore
Roses — Victoria Blakemore
Porcupines — Victoria Blakemore
Ice Cream — Victoria Blakemore

www.ingramcontent.com/pod-product-compliance
Lightning Source LLC
Chambersburg PA
CBHW051251020426

42333CB00025B/3155